THE OFFICIAL
CELTIC
ANNUAL 2014

Written by Joe Sullivan & Mark Henderson
Designed by Chris Dalrymple

THE CELTIC FOOTBALL CLUB
1888

A Grange Publication

© 2013. Published by Grange Communications Ltd., Edinburgh, under licence from Celtic Football Club. Printed in the EU.

ISBN 978-1-908925-38-1

£7.99

CONTENTS

CLUB HONOURS

Scottish League Winners [44 times]
1892/93, 1893/94, 1895/96, 1897/98, 1904/05, 1905/06, 1906/07, 1907/08, 1908/09, 1909/10, 1913/14, 1914/15, 1915/16, 1916/17, 1918/19, 1921/22, 1925/26, 1935/36, 1937/38, 1953/54, 1965/66, 1966/67, 1967/68, 1968/69, 1969/70, 1970/71, 1971/72, 1972/73, 1973/74, 1976/77, 1978/79, 1980/81,1981/82, 1985/86, 1987/88, 1997/98, 2000/01, 2001/02, 2003/04, 2005/06, 2006/07, 2007/08, 2011/12, 2012/13

Scottish Cup Winners [36 times]
1892, 1899, 1900, 1904, 1907, 1908, 1911, 1912, 1914, 1923, 1925, 1927, 1931, 1933, 1937, 1951, 1954, 1965, 1967, 1969, 1971, 1972, 1974, 1975, 1977, 1980, 1985, 1988, 1989, 1995, 2001, 2004, 2005, 2007, 2011, 2013

League Cup Winners [14 times]
1956/57, 1957/58, 1965/66, 1966/67, 1967/68, 1968/69, 1969/70, 1974/75, 1982/83, 1997/98, 1999/00, 2000/01, 2005/06, 2008/09

European Cup Winners 1967

Coronation Cup Winners 1953

MANAGER FACTFILE

D.O.B: 25/06/71

Born: Lurgan, Northern Ireland

Playing career record:

Manchester City (1989-90)
Crewe Alexandra (1990-96)
Leicester City (1996-2000)
Celtic (2000-07)
Nottingham Forest (2007-08)
Wycombe Wanderers (2008)

Playing honours:

Leicester City: League Cup Winners (1996/97, 1999/00)

Celtic: Scottish Premier League Champions: (2000/01, 2001/02, 2003/04, 2005/06, 2006/07)

Scottish Cup Winners (2001, 2004, 2005, 2007)

Scottish League Cup Winners: (2000/01, 2005/06)

UEFA Cup Runners-up: (2002/03)

As Manager:

Scottish Premier League Champions (2011/12, 2012/13)

Scottish Cup (2010/11, 2012/13)

NEIL LENNON

NEIL Lennon wrote himself into the history books last season by becoming only the third Celt to achieve the domestic double as both a player and manager, joining Jock Stein and Billy McNeill. To follow in the footsteps of two club legends was a very special moment for the Irishman.

Appointed interim manager in March 2010, he galvanised a team in turbulence to a respectable league finish after winning the eight remaining SPL games. That summer, he was handed the job on a permanent basis and quickly set about restoring Celtic as the dominant force in Scottish football.

In his first full season at the helm, he guided the Hoops to a Scottish Cup triumph courtesy of a convincing 3-0 victory over Motherwell. Celtic were back on the trophy trail and were unfortunate not to have savoured further success. Narrowly defeated after extra-time in the League Cup final, they were also in the running for the title until the last day of the season, only to suffer the agony of falling short by a single point.

Still, it had been 12 months of undoubted progress in Paradise as a youthful side captured the fans' imaginations with some exhilarating performances. Instead of deflation or despondency, there was a sense of optimism around the club again.

The championship had been absent from Paradise for three years and naturally that formed the main objective for Neil Lennon and his squad for the following season. After a stuttering start to the season, not helped by a lengthy injury list, it began to appear a distant dream.

However, Celtic dug deep and began to hit top form as winter approached. A magnificent 20-match run of victories in domestic football saw them overturn a 15-point deficit and storm to the SPL summit. At the start of April, they clinched the title in scintillating fashion with an emphatic 6-0 hammering of Kilmarnock.

While the Hoops came up short in the other domestic competitions, which included another League Cup final defeat, Neil Lennon was now a championship-winning manager and that made him immensely proud. Just over a month later, he got his hands on the trophy after a 5-0 demolition of Hearts at Celtic Park. Mission accomplished.

The task was now building on that success in the new season, particularly on the European front, a major aspiration for the Hoops boss. After successfully negotiating two challenging qualifiers against Helsinki and Helsingborgs, a return to the UEFA Champions League was secured for the first time since 2008.

Drawn in a group containing Barcelona, Benfica and Spartak Moscow, few expected the Scottish champions to qualify for the latter stages of the competition, but that is just what they did in an incredible campaign.

The highlight was undoubtedly a stunning 2-1 victory over the Catalan giants, widely regarded as the best team in the world. It was one of Celtic's greatest European results and a fitting way to celebrate the club's 125th

anniversary, which had been celebrated the previous evening in the place where it all began - St Mary's Church in the Calton.

Celtic eventually bowed out in the last 16 of the tournament to a slick Juventus outfit but it had been a fantastic adventure and had put the club back on the European map.

The physical and psychological toll of top-level continental competition had seen the Hoops search for consistency in domestic football in the opening months of the season but once that eased, they raced into a handsome lead at the top of the table.

It was only a matter of time before a second successive title was sealed and a resounding 4-1 victory over Inverness Caledonian Thistle in April confirmed Celtic's 44th league crown. The following month, the trophy was raised again in Paradise after another four-goal haul, this time St Johnstone were the victims.

Celtic could now fully focus on the Scottish Cup final against Hibernian in the season finale. A disappointing defeat in the League Cup semi-final had served to increase the team's determination to make amends at Hampden, and there never looked to be any doubt about the final outcome as the champions cruised to a convincing 3-0 triumph to lift the famous old trophy for the 36th time. Celtic were double winners and Neil Lennon had made history.

SEASON REVIEW

AUGUST

FOLLOWING games in Germany and matches against Ajax, Norwich City and Inter Milan, Celtic took to their first competitive action with gusto and finished the month of August at the top of the league despite having played a game fewer than second-placed Hibernian.

The reason for the discrepancy was that the Hoops flew over to the States to take on Real Madrid in Philadelphia following the opening weekend and by that time the Bhoys already had three wins in the bag.

Aside from the flag-day win over Aberdeen following the raising of the championship colours by club legend Sean Fallon, there were two wins over HJK Helsinki of Finland in the qualifiers for the UEFA Champions League.

The prize for negotiating the first European hurdle was another trip to Scandinavia, this time to Sweden, to take on Helsingborgs IF and once more the Bhoys won handsomely to qualify for the group stages of the world's foremost club competition.

As the month closed, the league leaders were drawn in Champions League Group G along with Spartak Moscow, Benfica and Catalan giants, Barcelona – very few people outside of Celtic Park gave the Hoops much hope of emerging from the group.

The name on everyone's lips when Celtic were paired with Helsingborgs IF was Hoops legend Henrik Larsson as he played with them before leaving his homeland and returned to play for them and finish his career there when he left Barcelona.

GOAL OF THE MONTH
Tony Wa
Invernes
Caledon
Thistle

AUGUST FIXTURES (Home fixtures in green)

01	UCL	2-1 v HJK Helsinki	(Hooper, Mulgrew)
04	SPL	1-0 v Aberdeen	(Commons)
08	UCL	2-0 v HJK Helsinki	(Ledley, Samaras)
18	SPL	1-1 v Ross County	(Commons)
21	UCL	2-0 v Helsingborgs	(Commons, Samaras)
25	SPL	4-2 v Inverness CT	(Mulgrew, Wanyama, Watt 2)
29	UCL	2-0 v Helsingborgs	(Wanyama, Hooper)

SEPTEMBER

CELTIC were still at the top of the table come the end of the second month of the campaign, despite not picking up full points in their first two games and still having played a game fewer than the chasing pack.

This time though, it was Motherwell who were leading the pack with the Fir Park side chasing just a point behind the Hoops and the champions had a 2-0 win down in Lanarkshire on the final card of the month to thank for their top placing as the Steelmen went into that game two points in front.

There was also an international break following the opening game of the month and the Hoops took to their first UEFA Champions League group stage game without talismanic striker Georgios Samaras, who had been on fine European goalscoring form.

The league campaign got back on track with the visit of SPL newcomers Dundee, who were defeated before Celtic opened up their League Cup campaign with the visit of Raith Rovers and the Fife side suffered at the feet of Gary Hooper who hit all of the home team's goals in a 4-1 win.

Then came that trip to Fir Park and the 2-0 win that ensured the Hoops would end another month at the top of the tree.

CELTIC CONNECTION

The Hoops met old foes Benfica for the fourth time in European competition and in previous meeting the ties had finished all square, but once more Celtic fans were delighted with another chance to visit Lisbon, the scene of the club's finest moment.

GOAL OF THE MONTH
Gary Hooper v Motherwell

SEPTEMBER FIXTURES (Home fixtures in green)			
01	SPL	2-2 v Hibernian	(Lustig, McPake og)
15	SPL	1-2 v St Johnstone	(Commons)
19	UCL	0-0 v Benfica	–
22	SPL	2-0 v Dundee	(Wanyama, Hooper)
25	SLC	4-1 v Raith Rovers	(Hooper 4)
29	SPL	2-0 v Motherwell	(Hooper, Cummins og)

OCTOBER

ONCE more the Hoops finished the month at the top of the league, but it was Hibernian who had climbed back to the number two spot and the Bhoys claimed top spot despite losing at home to Kilmarnock for the first time in over 50 years.

It was European football that kicked off October for the Bhoys and a visit to Russia delivered the club's first away win in the group stages of the UEFA Champions League when a last-gasp winner from Georgios Samaras took the spoils against Spartak Moscow on the artificial surface of the Luzhniki Stadium.

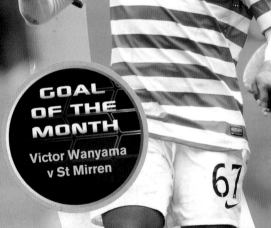

GOAL OF THE MONTH
Victor Wanyama v St Mirren

Samaras kept up his scoring form in the next game as his solitary goal brought Celtic all three points from the visit of Hearts and then the Hoops went on the road to hammer St Mirren 5-0 before flying out to take on the mighty Barcelona.

Once again, Samaras found the net as the Hoops took the lead after 18 minutes, but goals in the final seconds of each half denied Celtic at least a point against the Catalan giants as Celtic's European credibility rose once more.

Then followed the blip against Kilmarnock, but the Bhoys got back on track again and finished the month with a 5-0 win over St Johnstone.

OCTOBER FIXTURES (Home fixtures in green)

02	UCL	3-2 v Spartak Moscow	(Hooper, Kombarov og, Samaras)
07	SPL	1-0 v Hearts	(Samaras)
20	SPL	5-0 v St Mirren	(Wanyama 2, Ambrose, Hooper, Watt)
23	UCL	1-2 v Barcelona	(Samaras)
27	SPL	0-2 v Kilmarnock	–
30	SLC	5-0 v St Johnstone	(Commons 3, Hooper, Mulgrew)

NOVEMBER

CELTIC were on top of the world, never mind the top of the league, at the end of this month as they celebrated their 125th birthday in the best way possible by defeating the best club in the world in an unforgettable night in Paradise.

Just 24 hours before meeting Barcelona at Celtic Park, guests and dignitaries from both clubs took part in a special event at the club's birthplace, St Mary's Church in the Calton, and then a magnificent display from a packed Paradise greeted the players of the two great teams as they squared up to each other in the UEFA Champions League.

GOAL OF THE MONTH
Tony Watt v Barcelona

NOVEMBER FIXTURES (Home fixtures in green)

04	SPL	2-2 v Dundee United	(Watt, Miku)
07	UCL	2-1 v Barcelona	(Wanyama, Watt)
11	SPL	1-1 v St Johnstone	(Watt)
17	SPL	2-0 v Aberdeen	(Lassad, Mulgrew)
20	UCL	1-2 v Benfica	(Samaras)
24	SPL	0-1 v Inverness CT	–
28	SPL	4-0 v Hearts	(Lustig, Lassad, Hooper, Stevenson og)

CELTIC CONNECTION

The Hoops marked their 125th Anniversary in fine style by beating Barca and eventually winning the double – on their 50th Anniversary, Celtic won the title and, of course, lifted the double in the club's Centenary Year.

Victor Wanyama headed Celtic into the lead on 21 minutes before teenager Tony Watt came off the bench and fired himself into the Celtic history books when he made it 2-0 on 83 minutes. The striker latched on to a long clearance from Fraser Forster and held his nerve to slot the ball beyond Victor Valdes in the Barca goal.

Not even an injury-time goal from Lionel Messi could take any shine off of a magnificent victory and a result which reverberated throughout the football world.

Even the fact that the historic win was sandwiched by two domestic draws could not take the sheen from a magnificent night in the club's history and, despite losing 2-1 to Benfica in the next European game, qualifying from the group remained a distinct possibility.

GOAL OF THE MONTH
Georgios Samaras v Kilmarnock

CELTIC CONNECTION

The Hoops were caused problems by Second Division Arbroath, but in 1993 they met the same side in the League Cup when the Gayfield side were managed by Celtic legend Danny McGrain. However, on that occasion the Bhoys racked up a 9-1 scoreline.

DECEMBER

CELTIC finished off 2012 further ahead at the top of the league, despite losing the final game of the calendar year to Hibernian at Easter Road and the month didn't get off to the best of starts either with a 1-1 draw at home to Arbroath in the Scottish Cup.

Battling Arbroath were beaten in the replay later in the month and the Hoops picked up full SPL points elsewhere in a rather productive month as they finished six points ahead of both Inverness Caledonian Thistle and Motherwell – plus they still had a game in hand over

The big talking point of the month, though, came in just the second game when, only four days after drawing with lowly Arbroath, Celtic hosted Spartak Moscow in the final Group G game knowing that they had to better Benfica's score against Barcelona in the other game to progress to the last 16.

The Hoops went into the game with a winning mentality – and they had to as the Portuguese side were holding Barcelona at 0-0 but Spartak had pulled the Celtic Park game back to 1-1 after Gary Hooper had opened the scoring earlier in the match.

However, in the 82nd minute, Celtic were awarded a penalty and Kris Commons duly fired home to send the Hoops into the last

JANUARY

BY the end of this month the Hoops had surged to a 15-point lead at the top of the tree with both Inverness Caledonian Thistle and Motherwell trailing on 37 points to Celtic's 52 as the second successive championship now loomed in sight.

That was thanks to four straight SPL wins that traversed the winter break with the Bhoys heading off to the sunnier climes of Spain after getting the year 2013 off to a good start with a 1-0 win over Motherwell at home.

The Hoops racked up 13 goals in their four SPL matches with Gary Hooper scoring five of those, but the English striker also scored in another match that wasn't destined to deliver further success to Celtic.

CELTIC CONNECTION

Welsh wonders Joe Ledley and Adam Matthews scored three goals between them in the 4-1 defeat of Kilmarnock, but they still had some way to go to compete with fellow countryman John Hartson – Big Bad John scored no fewer than five hat-tricks for Celtic, including a four-goal haul in a 7-0 win over Aberdeen.

GOAL OF THE MONTH
Adam Matthews v Kilmarnock

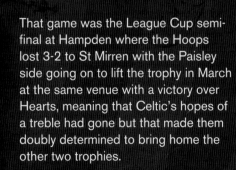

That game was the League Cup semi-final at Hampden where the Hoops lost 3-2 to St Mirren with the Paisley side going on to lift the trophy in March at the same venue with a victory over Hearts, meaning that Celtic's hopes of a treble had gone but that made them doubly determined to bring home the other two trophies.

The double was still very much on and the Bhoys in green and white still had an interest in European football after the turn of the year as well.

JANUARY FIXTURES (Home fixtures in green)

02	SPL	1-0 v Motherwell	(Hooper)
19	SPL	4-1 v Hearts	(Hooper 2, Samaras, Lassad)
22	SPL	4-0 v Dundee United	(Hooper2, Wanyama, Brown)
27	LC	2-3 v St Mirren	(Hooper, Mulgrew)
30	SPL	4-1 v Kilmarnock	(Ledley, Matthews 2, Stokes)

FEBRUARY

CELTIC ended this month a cool 19 points ahead at the top of the table despite losing to second-placed Motherwell in February's final game, but the month got off to a great start when the Hoops strengthened their double ambitions against Raith Rovers in the Scottish Cup.

The Bhoys travelled through to Fife and returned with a 3-0 win under their belts with the Kirkcaldy result setting them up for a similar result a week later when their travels took them further afield to record a 3-1 win over Inverness Caledonian Thistle.

The big game came in midweek, though, as Italian giants Juventus visited Celtic Park on UEFA Champions League duty and, despite Celtic dominating for much of the game, it was the visitors who delivered the killer blows with goals from Alessandro Matri, Claudio Marchisio and Mirko Vucinic giving the Turin side a 3-0 win.

However, far from being jaded on their return to domestic action, the Hoops rallied and hammered Dundee United 6-2 while a midweek blip of a 1-1 draw with St Johnstone was remedied with another landslide against the other Tayside club when Dundee were beaten 5-0.

Celtic's grip on the title just got tighter following another successful month for the Bhoys in green and white.

GOAL OF THE MONTH
Gary Hooper v Dundee

CELTIC CONNECTION

The Hoops were meeting old adversaries Juventus for the third time in European competition, the first of those coming in the 1981/82 season when future Celtic manager Liam Brady was a star player for the Italian club.

FEBRUARY FIXTURES (Home fixtures in green)

02	SC	3-0 v Raith Rovers	(Commons, Forrest, Mulgrew)
09	SPL	3-1 v Inverness CT	(Commons, Gershon, Miku)
12	UCL	0-3 v Juventus	–
16	SPL	6-2 v Dundee United	(Ambrose, Commons 2, Ledley, Stokes 3)
19	SPL	1-1 v St Johnstone	(Ambrose)
24	SPL	5-0 v Dundee	(Ledley 2, Forrest, McGeouch, Hooper)
27	SPL	1-2 v Motherwell	(Samaras)

MARCH

ONCE more, Scottish Cup action kicked off the month and this time Celtic gained some sort of revenge for their earlier League Cup exit at the hands of St Mirren as this time the side visited Paisley in hope of progress in their bid for world football's oldest trophy.

The scoring was concluded by the 21st minute as Celtic won 2-1 and progressed to a semi-final meeting with Dundee United at the National Stadium, but there was still plenty to be taken care of before that Hampden date.

Next up was Juventus in Turin and a 2-0 win for the Italian giants ended Celtic's slim hopes of further progress in that competition but Neil Lennon's Hoops went out with their heads held high and returned to concentrate on domestic matters.

There were further slips, but a loss at Ross County and a draw with St Mirren on the road, sandwiched one of the most amazing games of the season when Aberdeen visited Celtic Park on league duty.

Kris Commons scored the SPL's quickest ever goal when he found the net after 12 seconds. However, with half an hour left, Aberdeen were leading 3-1 before the Bhoys pulled it back to 3-3. Just when most people would have settled for that comeback, Georgios Samaras capped it all with an overhead kick in the 94th minute to record a 4-3 victory.

GOAL OF THE MONTH
Georgios Samaras v Aberdeen

CELTIC CONNECTION

The last-minute goal against Aberdeen was all part of the eventual double success in the club's 125th year but last-gasp winning goals were a regular feature in many games of the centenary double achievements of season 1987/88.

MARCH FIXTURES (Home fixtures in green)			
02	SC	2-1 v St Mirren	(Ledley, Stokes)
06	UCL	0-2 v Juventus	–
09	SPL	2-3 v Ross County	(Mulgrew, Hooper)
16	SPL	4-3 v Aberdeen	(Commons, Hooper, Mulgrew, Samaras)
31	SPL	1-1 v St Mirren	(Commons)

APRIL

THIS is the month when the champions-elect became the champions for real and, after beating Hibernian 3-0 in the opening game of the month, the Bhoys knew it was in their hands in the next SPL game and they knew exactly what they had to do.

In between times, though, there was the small matter of the Scottish Cup semi-final and maintaining the drive for double silverware with an in-form Dundee United standing between Celtic and another Hampden season-finale.

Just 24 hours previously, a watching TV audience experienced a thrilling end-to-end game in which Hibernian finally saw off Falkirk by 4-3 after extra-time – surely the other semi-final couldn't live up to that?

Well, there was just as much drama with the same extra-time scoreline from Celtic and United as the action swayed from one end of Hampden to the other with Anthony Stokes' final goal ensuring that the double was still on.

The following week, Inverness Caledonian Thistle arrived at Celtic Park with their eyes still set on Europe – while a win for Celtic would mean only one thing – the championship!

All of the goals in the clinching 4-1 win arrived in the second half and when, due to a touchline ban, Neil Lennon appeared 15 minutes after the final whistle, the championship celebrations could begin in earnest.

GOAL OF THE MONTH
Georgios Samaras v St Johnstone

CELTIC CONNECTION

The Hoops ding-dong battle with Dundee United in the Scottish Cup semi-final almost went to penalties. That would have brought back memories of the League Cup semi-final of 2009 when Celtic eventually beat United 11-10 on penalties –with both keepers, Artur Boruc and Lukasz Zaluska, then with United, taking spot kicks.

APRIL FIXTURES (Home fixtures in green)			
06	SPL	3-0 v Hibernian	(Lustig, Commons 2)
14	SC	4-3 v Dundee United	(Commons 2, Wanyama, Stokes)
21	SPL	4-1 v Inverness CT	(Hooper 2, Ledley, Samaras)
28	SPL	1-3 v Motherwell	(Hooper)

Celtic Football Club
Clydesdale Bank
Premier League
Champions 2012/13

GOAL OF THE MONTH

Joe Ledley v St Johnstone

MAY

THE merry and magnificently memorable month of May wasn't going to be spoiled by the opening 1-1 draw with Ross County up in Dingwall, as a young Celtic side was fielded as Neil Lennon weighed-up his options for the upcoming Scottish Cup final.

Before that, though, there was the thoroughly engrossing matter of the SPL trophy presentation and the Hoops made it a day to remember before and after the final whistle as they racked up a 4-0 win over the visiting St Johnstone side to round off the season in some style.

Another 4-0 victory, this time over Dundee United at Tannadice, pulled the curtain down on Celtic's triumphant SPL campaign meaning that there was just one game left – the Scottish Cup final where Hibernian stood between Celtic and their dream of the double in their 125th Anniversary year.

The cup and the double were won on a glorious day at Hampden with Gary Hooper scoring twice along with another from Joe Ledley ensuring that Neil Lennon became the seventh Celtic manager to lift the double and the third after Jock Stein and Billy McNeill to lift the double as both player and manager.

It was the ideal way to finish off the club's 125th season against the side whose first Scottish Cup win sowed the seeds of Celtic's birth.

CELTIC CONNECTION

The Scottish Cup final win against Hibernian was Celtic's 36th to add to their 44th championship meaning that 15 doubles have been won along the way.

WINNERS 2013

MAY FIXTURES (Home fixtures in green)

05	SPL	1-1 v Ross County	(Stokes)
11	SPL	4-0 v St Johnstone	(Ledley, Forrest, Mulgrew, Wright OG)
19	SPL	4-0 v Dundee United	(Commons, Samaras 2, Stokes)
26	SC	3-0 v Hibernian (Final)	(Hooper 2, Ledley)

17

Celtic Soccer Skills School

Learn the tricks of the trade from the best in the business.

KRIS COMMONS – PENALTY KICKS

TAKING a penalty kick can appear a daunting prospect, especially when there is much at stake and the pressure is on.

But with proper preparation and plenty of practice, you can become deadly from 12 yards – and that is a valuable asset to any side.

Over the years, Celtic have had some brilliant exponents in this part of the game such as Lisbon Lion Tommy Gemmell and John Collins.

One of the recent penalty kings in Paradise is Kris Commons, and here the attacker reveals his four top tips on how to be successful from the spot:

Don't change your mind

If you are the designated penalty taker, you should think about where you are going to put one even before putting your kit on for the game. When that is set in your mind, it's half the battle. When preparing for a game, you are thinking about how you are going to play and impose yourself on the match and you should also be thinking about where you will put a penalty kick. Once you have decided, don't change your mind.

Focus on striking the ball cleanly

I wouldn't advise trying to send the keeper the wrong way. For me, power is my strength so I try to make a good connection on the ball and strike through it where I am aiming and wanting the ball to go. I wouldn't think about watching the goalkeeper, trying to send him the wrong way and wanting to be all fancy. Just pick a spot, have a good connection and strike through the ball.

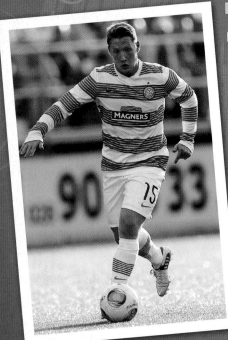

Practice makes perfect

It's important to practice your penalties in training and not just into an empty goal. Try to have a goalkeeper in there and get used to hitting that same spot as practice does make perfect, especially in this instance.

Follow a routine

I make it the exact same as I would do in training. Follow the same schedule. When you put the ball down and aren't sure what you are going do, that's when you start getting nervous and all your problems start. So have a bit of a routine. I always place the ball down, have a few deep breaths, clear my studs and make sure my shin pads are up. I then pick my spot, never change my mind and strike as confidently as I can.

ON THE SPOT IN PARADISE

Talk us through the penalty you scored against Spartak Moscow that sent Celtic into the last 16 of the UEFA Champions League.

"As I said before, when you take a penalty it's important that you clear your studs and follow the rest of your routine – think about what you do in training. So that is what I did:

"I put the ball down, took a few deep breaths and calmed myself down and then looked at the goalkeeper.

"He was a big guy and I had missed a penalty down the middle before because I didn't go high enough so I made sure I did that this time, and lucky for me it went high but not too much.

"Within a matter of milliseconds of it leaving my foot it hits the bar and goes in. And it was a wipe the sweat off your brow moment. I was delighted it went in."

EUROVISION

CELTIC celebrated 50 years of participating in European competition last season in style with their memorable run to the last 16 of the UEFA Champions League.

The victory over Barcelona in the group stages was one of the greatest nights in the club's history and a fitting way to celebrate the club's 125th anniversary, which fell on the previous day.

All supporters have their favourite memories from clashes with continental opposition and we quizzed the players on their highlights – see if any of them match yours.

Emilio Izaguirre

First European match?

I missed all the European matches two seasons ago because I was injured, so my first match was at home in the Champions League qualifier against Helsinki last season.

Favourite European ground?

Celtic Park, but away from home it would be the Camp Nou, but only with the Celtic fans there as well.

A Champions League final you enjoyed watching?

Barcelona when they beat Manchester United 3-1 at Wembley in 2011. Messi and Pedro scored in the game and it's one I really liked watching.

A European city you have played in with Celtic and would like to return to?

I liked Barcelona. We were playing against the best team in Europe and it's good to play against good teams. It was a nice city as well and the language was better for me also!

A European team you have not faced yet but would like to play against?

I would really like to play against Manchester United.

Hardest opponent you have come up against in Europe?

Every team is hard to play in Europe. All the big teams have good players and that makes them very hard to play against – Barcelona, Real Madrid and Bayern Munich, they are all the same. The best player I have faced, though, was Aiden McGeady at Spartak. He was a very good player and hard to play against, but I tried my best.

Greatest European game you have been involved in?

The Spartak Moscow at home when we won 2-1 and qualified for the last 16 of the Champions League. That is a very good memory.

Georgios Samaras

First European match?

Against Lierse from Belgium when I was with Heerenveen. It was in the Intertoto Cup and it was at home. We won 4-1 and I was only 17. We reached the final that year but lost to Villarreal.

Favourite European ground?

The Camp Nou because it's the home of Barcelona, simple as that.

A Champions League final you enjoyed watching?

The best one I have seen in the last couple of years was Liverpool against AC Milan in Istanbul. That was a great game and it was a wonderful game to watch on TV. But I was at the AC Milan v Liverpool final a few years later in Athens when AC Milan won 2-1 with two goals from Inzaghi. Because I was inside the ground and could feel the atmosphere, it was incredible.

A European city you have played in with Celtic and would like to return to?

I haven't played there in a European game, but there is only one city I would want to go back to and that is my hometown, Heraklion in Crete.

A European team you have not faced but would like to play against?

Real Madrid – we seem to always draw Barcelona in the Champions League!

Hardest opponent you have come up against in Europe?

Barcelona are the best team I have faced by a long way and Messi the best player. He can really do anything but we stopped them at home.

Greatest European game you have been involved in?

That's an easy answer, beating Barcelona.

To find the EuroVision answers of Joe Ledley and Adam Matthews turn to pages 48/49.

SPOT THE DIFFERENCE

THERE are 12 differences between these pictures of Joe Ledley in action in against Barcelona in the Nou Camp. The first one has been circled, but can you spot the rest?

Answers on pages 62/63.

SPL SEASON 2012/13 QUIZ

01 How many league titles have Celtic now won?

02 How many goals did Celtic score during the campaign?

03 And how many of those were own goals by the opposition?

04 Against which side did Celtic start the SPL campaign?

05 Celtic scored six goals in a game against which SPL side?

06 Which side failed to score against Celtic during the campaign?

07 How many clean sheets did Celtic record in the title run?

08 Who scored Celtic's first goal of the campaign?

09 Against which side did Celtic clinch the title?

10 Which Celt scored on his SPL debut?

How did you do? Find out with the answers on pages 62/63.

Manager's Office

Home Dressing Room

DOUBLE DEBUTS... AS PLAYER AND MANAGER

DAVIE HAY'S debut as a player was against Aberdeen as a substitute at home in the league with a 4-1 win on March 6, 1968, in front of a crowd of 28,000 with goals by Bobby Lennox (3) and Billy McNeill. As manager it was against Brechin City away in the League Cup in a 1-0 win thanks to a goal from Jim Melrose in front of a 3,000 crowd on August 2, 1983.

TOMMY BURNS' debut as a player was against Dundee at home in the league as a sub in a 2-1 defeat watched by 13,000 on April 19, 1975, with Celtic's goal scored by Ronnie Glavin. As manager it was a 1-1 league draw at Falkirk with Andy Walker scoring the Celtic goal in front of 12,200 on August 13, 1994.

EVER wondered what a Celtic player's CV would be like? Well, we've posed some questions to a few players to see what their answers are.

We've found out how they have progressed as players, what they feel they need to improve on and we also discover a few secrets....

DYLAN McGEOUCH

Where did you hone your football skills as a youngster?

I didn't really play for a lot of youth teams. I played for my primary school team in Milton, St Augustine's and then played for my local team, Glasgow Perthshire. After that, I went into the Celtic Development Centre up at the Science Park and started training up there.

Biggest influence?

Probably my Dad. He took me and my older brother to every training session and game, and that was all over the country as well. He dedicated a lot of his time to us and it's good to pay him back by playing for the team he has supported all his life.

What is your greatest strength as a footballer?

Attacking play, obviously I am an attack-minded player and not really defensive, so going forward with the ball.

Anything you feel you could improve in your game?

You are never 100 percent with everything, so you can always improve in every aspect of your game but there are obvious things like working on your weaker foot.

Tell us something about yourself that we don't already know?

When I was younger, I used to be a ball-boy at Celtic Park. I remember being at Celtic v Rangers games and celebrating behind the goal on Champions League nights, including the game when Shunsuke Nakamura scored the free-kick against Manchester United.

Proudest achievement on football CV?

Scoring the Goal of the Season on my home debut at Celtic Park. That is my biggest achievement and favourite memory so far.

Why did you want to join Celtic?

I grew up supporting Celtic and my family are massive Celtic fans. I was here at first and when I had the chance to come back, it was a no-brainer as I am huge fan of the club. To have the opportunity of playing in the Celtic first team was massive so I had to take it.

Most important ingredient in becoming a successful footballer?

Obviously you need to have good talent but hunger as well – to get better, improve your game and put the hard work in.

What interests do you have outside of football?

I like watching snooker and have been going to that recently. I also used to go fishing quite a lot, so both of those.

What job would like to do if you weren't a footballer?

Probably an English and Maths teacher, as I am that smart!

Tell us one fact about Celtic.

Best fans in the world. Growing up and watching Celtic all over the world and seeing the support they take away both at home and abroad and there is nothing like the atmosphere at Celtic Park on the Champions League nights.

LUKASZ ZALUSKA

Where did you hone your football skills as a youngster?

In the beginning, I played in my home city at a lower division club, but when I was 15 I moved 400 miles away to attend a goalkeeping school called MSP. It is the most famous goalkeeping school in Poland and is the same place Fabianski at Arsenal went to. I was away from my family and had goalkeeping sessions every day.

Biggest influence?

Probably the goalkeeping coach at the goalkeeping school I went to – Andrzej Dawidziuk, who is now the goalkeeping coach for the Polish national team. He taught me a lot, from all the simple things at the beginning. I spent three years training every day with him.

What is your greatest strength as a footballer?

It's hard to say, you would need to ask Woodsy! (Stevie Woods, Celtic's goalkeeping coach)

Anything you feel you could improve in your game?

Probably my kicking – you can always do better when you are a footballer.

Tell us something about yourself that we don't already know?

I am a massive fan of sharks! I love to watch documentary movies about them on channels like National Geographic. My dream is to go to South Africa and dive in the cage with the Great White Shark, as you can do that there. That is my dream and I am going to do it in the next few years. I just love sharks.

Proudest achievement on football CV?

To play for my national team and to win two championships and two Scottish Cups with Celtic.

Why did you want to join Celtic?

To be honest, since coming to Scotland that was my plan: every game for me was a chance to try and get the Celtic scouts interested in me as they are the biggest club in Scotland. Artur Boruc, my fellow Polish goalkeeper, was also here and he was my friend. I spoke with him a lot about Celtic and I knew how big this club is.

Most important ingredient in becoming a successful footballer?

Hard work, character and a lot of luck.

What interests do you have outside of football?

I just love to watch any kind of movies. During the season we spend around three nights a week in a hotel, so we have plenty of time to watch movies and I always kill my free time watching films.

What job would like to do if you weren't a footballer?

I would probably do something that is a different discipline of football, like volleyball or handball, which is a really big sport in Poland. I love sport, and I can't imagine never playing football, but if it happened I would go for another sport.

Tell us one fact about Celtic.

I know that Celtic took the largest-ever travelling support overseas for the UEFA Cup final in Seville. I spoke with my Scottish friend and he went over there with his son and told me all the stories, how there was plane after plane leaving from Glasgow full of Celtic fans. He said it was one of the best days in his life. Although the score wasn't good, he said the atmosphere was great and Glasgow Airport was something magic. He said there was something like 40,000 Celtic fans inside the stadium and another 40,000 outside around the city. I would have loved to have been part of this.

To read the CVs of Mikael Lustig and John Herron, turn to pages 40/41.

AFTER having an amazing performance for the Hoops at Paradise, James Forrest had to go up to Sponsors' Lounge to pick up his Man of the Match award.

Can you help him get upstairs for his award by finding the proper route through the maze?

Find out how James gets up to the presentation on pages 62/63.

QUIZ QUESTIONS

01 How many times have Celtic won the League Cup?

02 And how many times have the Hoops won the Scottish Cup?

03 Which Celt scored the opening goal in the 2-1 win over Barcelona?

04 Against which side did Celtic kick-off the 2012/13 European campaign?

05 In which month during the season did Celtic play the most games?

Check out the answers on pages 62/63.

WORDSEARCH

01 Home country of Emilio Izaguirre.

02 Nickname of Celtic Park.

03 James Forrest's number.

04 Celtic's 2013 Scottish Cup final opponents.

05 Home town of Georgios Samaras.

06 Club we signed Lukasz Zaluska from.

07 They score most of the goals.

08 The last line of defence.

09 Celtic won this in Lisbon.

Answers on pages 62/63

H	R	G	W	M	J	R	F	Q	E	L	D	W
E	H	Y	J	F	W	Z	K	S	H	E	Q	T
R	M	I	K	B	C	V	I	L	T	Q	V	X
A	N	Y	B	M	P	D	S	I	D	M	T	T
K	T	L	J	E	A	T	N	M	R	K	L	S
L	J	T	M	R	R	U	T	Y	T	N	N	A
I	R	L	A	I	E	N	C	D	N	K	X	R
O	Z	P	K	E	F	B	I	Z	V	K	Z	U
N	T	E	D	X	G	L	X	A	B	Y	P	D
J	R	N	R	M	H	N	K	V	N	M	V	N
S	U	Z	F	O	R	T	Y	N	I	N	E	O
D	E	U	R	O	P	E	A	N	C	U	P	H
R	E	P	E	E	K	L	A	O	G	G	G	R

Manager's Office

Home Dressing Room

DOUBLE DEBUTS... AS PLAYER AND MANAGER

BILLY McNEILL'S debut as a player was against Clyde in the League Cup at home in a 2-0 win on August 23, 1958, with goals by Sammy Wilson and Bertie Auld watched by a crowd of 39,000. As manager, it was against Morton away in the league in a 2-1 win with goals by Ronnie Glavin and Roddy MacDonald in front of a 16,000 crowd on August 12, 1978. On his return as manager, it was again against Morton away in the league in a 4-0 win with goals by Andy Walker (2), Mark McGhee, and Billy Stark in front of 15,500 on August 8, 1987.

JOCK STEIN'S debut as a player was against St Mirren in the league at home in a 2-1 win on December 8, 1951, with both goals scored by Jim Lafferty in front of 20,000. As manager, it was against Airdrie away in the league on March 10, 1965, in a 6-0 win watched by 18,000 with the goals coming from Bertie Auld (5) and John Hughes.

CELTIC'S GOT TALENT

SCOTT BROWN

Position: Midfielder
Squad Number: 8
D.O.B: 25/06/85
Born: Hill o' Beath, Scotland
Height: 5'10"
Signed: 29/05/07
Debut: v Kilmarnock (h) 0-0 (SPL) 05/08/07
Previous Clubs: Hibernian

GEORGIOS SAMARAS

Position: Centre-forward
Squad Number: 9
D.O.B: 21/02/85
Born: Heraklion, Greece
Height: 6'4"
Signed: 29/01/08
Debut: v Kilmarnock (a) 5-1 (SC) 02/02/08
Previous Clubs: Manchester City, Heerenveen

FRASER FORSTER

Position: Goalkeeper
Squad Number: 1
D.O.B: 17/03/88
Born: Hexham, England
Height: 6'7"
Signed: 01/08/10
Debut: v Motherwell (a) 1-0 (SPL) 29/08/10
Previous Clubs: Newcastle United, Norwich City (loan), Bristol Rovers (loan), Stockport County (loan)

LUKASZ ZALUSKA

Position: Goalkeeper
Squad Number: 24
D.O.B: 16/06/82
Born: Wysokie Mazowieckie, Poland
Height: 6'4"
Signed: 01/06/09
Debut: v Falkirk (a) 4-0 (LC) 23/09/09
Previous Clubs: Dundee United, Korona Kielce, Legia Warsaw, Stomil Olsztyn, Zryw Zielona Gora, Sparta Obornoki, MSP Szamotuly, Ruch Wysokie Mazowieckie

JAMES FORREST

Position: Winger
Squad: 49
D.O.B: 07/07/91
Born: Glasgow, Scotland
Height: 5'9"
Signed: 30/08/09
Debut: v Motherwell (h) 4-0 (SPL) 01/05/10
Previous Clubs: Celtic Youth

BERAM KAYAL

Position: Midfielder
Squad Number: 33
D.O.B: 02/05/88
Born: Jadeidi, Israel
Height: 5'10"
Signed: 29/07/10
Debut: v FC Utrecht (h) 2-0, (EL) 19/08/10
Previous Clubs: Maccabi Haifa

CELTIC'S GOT TALENT

CHARLIE MULGREW

Position: Defender
Squad Number: 21
D.O.B: 06/03/86
Born: Glasgow, Scotland
Height: 6'2"
Signed: 01/07/10
Debut: v SC Braga (a) 0-3, (UCL) 28/07/10
Previous Clubs: Aberdeen, Southend (loan), Wolves, Dundee United (loan), Celtic

JOE LEDLEY

Position: Midfielder
Squad Number: 16
D.O.B: 23/01/87
Born: Cardiff, Wales
Height: 6'0"
Signed: 12/07/10
Debut: v SC Braga (a) 0-3, (UCL) 28/07/10
Previous Clubs: Cardiff City

MARCUS FRASER

Position: Defender
Squad Number: 44
D.O.B: 23/06/94
Born: Bishopbriggs, Scotland
Height: 5'11"
Signed: 01/08/10
Debut: v Rennes (h) 3-1, (EL) 03/11/11
Previous Clubs: Celtic Youth

EMILIO IZAGUIRRE

Position: **Defender**
Squad Number: **3**
D.O.B: **10/05/86**
Born: **Tegucigalpa, Honduras**
Height: **5'8"**
Signed: **18/08/10**
Debut: **v Motherwell (a) 1-0, (SPL) 29/08/10**
Previous Clubs: **Motagua**

KRIS COMMONS

Position: **Midfielder**
Squad Number: **15**
D.O.B: **30/08/83**
Born: **Nottingham, England**
Height: **5'6"**
Signed: **28/01/11**
Debut: **v Aberdeen (h) 4-1, (CIS) 29/01/11**
Previous Clubs: **Derby County, Nottingham Forest, Stoke City**

ANTHONY STOKES

Position: **Striker**
Squad Number: **10**
D.O.B: **25/07/88**
Born: **Dublin, Ireland**
Height: **5'11"**
Signed: **31/08/10**
Debut: **v Hearts (h) 3-0, (SPL) 11/09/11**
Previous Clubs: **Hibernian, Crystal Palace (loan), Sheffield United (loan), Sunderland, Falkirk (loan), Arsenal**

CELTIC'S GOT TALENT

ADAM MATTHEWS

Position: Defender
Squad Number: 2
D.O.B: 13/01/92
Born: Swansea, Wales
Height: 5'10"
Signed: 01/07/11
Debut: v Aberdeen (a) 1-0, (SPL) 07/08/11
Previous Clubs: Cardiff City

BAHRUDIN ATAJIC

Position: Attacker
Squad Number: 37
D.O.B: 16/11/93
Born: Vastervik, Sweden
Height: 6'4"
Signed: 20/01/2010
Debut: Dundee United (a) 4-0 19/05/13
Previous Clubs: Malmo

DYLAN McGEOUCH

Position: Midfielder
Squad Number: 46
D.O.B: 15/01/93
Born: Glasgow, Scotland
Height: 5'10"
Signed: 01/06/11
Debut: v Motherwell (a) 2-1, (SPL) 06/11/11
Previous Clubs: Rangers Youth, Celtic Youth

FILIP TWARDZIK

Position: Midfielder
Squad Number: 56
D.O.B: 10/02/93
Born: Trinec, Czech Republic
Height: 6'2"
Signed: 31/01/09
Debut: v Peterhead (a) 3-0, (SC) 08/01/12
Previous Clubs: Hertha BSC , Sachsen Leipzig,

JOHN HERRON

Position: Midfielder
Squad Number: 31
D.O.B: 1/02/94
Born: Bellshill, Scotland
Height: 6'0"
Signed: 12/07/10
Debut: Ross County (h) 4-0, (SPL) 22/12/12
Previous Clubs: Celtic Youth

MIKAEL LUSTIG

Position: Right-back
Squad Number: 23
D.O.B: 13/12/86
Born: Umea, Sweden
Height: 6'2"
Signed: 01/01/12
Debut: v Aberdeen (a) 1-1, (SPL) 03/03/12
Previous Clubs: Rosenborg, GIF Sundsvall, Umea, Sandakerms SK

CELTIC'S GOT T★LENT

PAUL GEORGE

Position: Winger
Squad Number: 50
D.O.B: 27/01/94
Born: Killough, Ireland
Height: 5'8"
Signed: 01/08/11
Debut: v Ross County (a) 2-0, League Cup 21/11/11
Previous Clubs: Celtic Youth

TONY WATT

Position: Striker
Squad Number: 32
D.O.B: 29/12/93
Born: Coatbridge, Scotland
Height: 6'0"
Signed: 04/01/2011
Debut: v Motherwell (a) 3-0, (SPL) 22/04/12
Previous Clubs: Airdrie United

TOM ROGIC

Position: Midfielder
Squad Number: 18
D.O.B: 16/12/92
Born: Griffith, Australia
Height: 6'2"
Signed: 09/01/13
Debut: v Inverness Caledonian Thistle (a) 3-1, (SPL) 09/02/13
Previous Clubs: Central Coast Mariners, Belconnen United, ANU FC

EFE AMBROSE

Position: Defender
Squad Number: 4
D.O.B: 18/10/88
Born: Kaduna, Nigeria
Height: 6' 3"
Signed: 31/08/12
Debut: Dundee (h) 2-0, (SPL) 22/09/12
Previous Clubs: FC Ashdod, Kaduna United

JOE CHALMERS

Position: Defender
Squad Number: 43
D.O.B: 03/01/94
Born: Rutherglen, Scotland
Height: 6'1"
Signed: 12/07/10
Debut: Inverness (a) 4-2, (SPL) 25/0812
Previous Clubs: Celtic Youth

JACKSON IRVINE

Position: Midfielder
Squad Number: 36
D.O.B: 07/03/93
Born: Melbourne, Australia
Height: 6'2"
Signed: 19/11/10
Debut: Hibernian (h) 2-2, (SPL) 01/09/12
Previous Clubs:

CELTIC'S GOT TALENT

AMIDO BALDE

Position: Attacker
Squad Number: 17
D.O.B: 16/05/91
Born: Bissau, Guinea-Bissau
Height: 6'4"
Signed: 13/06/13
Debut: Cliftonville (h), 2-0, (UCL), 23/07/13
Previous Clubs: Sporting Lisbon, Santa Clara, Badajoz, Cercle Brugge, Vitoria Guimaraes

VIRGIL VAN DIJK

Position: Defender
Squad Number: 5
D.O.B: 08/07/91
Born: Breda, Netherlands
Height: 6'4"
Signed: 21/06/13
Debut: Aberdeen (a) 2-0, (SPFL) 17/08/13
Previous Clubs: Willem II, FC Groningen

STEVEN MOUYOKOLO

Position: Defender
Squad Number: 22
D.O.B: 24/01/87
Born: Melun, France
Height: 6'3"
Signed: 15/07/13
Debut: Aberdeen (a) 2-0, (SPFL) 17/08/13
Previous Clubs: Sochaux (loan), Wolverhampton Wanderers, Hull City, Boulogne, Gueugnon, Chateauroux

DERK BOERRIGTER

Position: Attacker
Squad Number: 11
D.O.B: 16/10/86
Born: Oldenzaal, Netherlands
Height: 6'4"
Signed: 30/06/13
Debut: Ross County (h) 2-1, (SPFL) 03/08/13
Previous Clubs: Ajax, Haarlem (loan), Zwolle, RKC Waalwijk, Ajax

TEEMU PUKKI

Position: Attacker
Squad Number: 20
D.O.B: 29/03/90
Born: Kotka, Finland
Height: 5'11"
Signed: 31/08/13
Debut:
Previous Clubs: FC KooTeePee, Sevilla Atletico, Sevilla, HJK, Schalke 04

NIR BITON

Position: Midfielder
Squad Number: 6
D.O.B: 30/10/91
Born: Ashdod, Israel
Height: 6'5"
Signed: 30/08/13
Debut:
Previous Clubs: FC Ashdod

Celtic Soccer Skills School

Learn the tricks of the trade from the best in the business.

WING-PLAY – JAMES FORREST

THERE is nothing more exciting in football than watching a wide-player wreaking havoc on an opposition defence.

When the route to goal is congested, they can provide a moment of magic to conjure up a chance for others or themselves, whether through a piece of skill, a dangerous delivery or a burst of speed.

Celtic fans have always held a special affection for these types of players – the likes of Jimmy Johnstone, Charlie Tully and Bobby Lennox were all firm favourites in Paradise.

The latest wing wizard to grace the Hoops is Youth Academy graduate, James Forrest, who has proven his ability on the big stage for club and country since breaking into the first team.

Here are his top skills to learn to become successful in this important position.

Crossing the ball

If you have the time, have a look up and see who is in the box. If you aren't able to do that, just try and hit a good area in the box and hopefully one of the strikers can get on the end of it. You can either stand it up to the back post or try and whip it in to the near post and then hopefully someone in the box can finish it off.

For home games, I preview the game in the studio with Mark Henderson or Laura Brannan from the *Celtic View* before commentating on the game with Paul Cuddihy. Away games are slightly different as I am in the studio myself back in the stadium and this allows me to correspond with all the fans abroad. We get lots of e-mails as well, which is really pleasing and you get a real sense of the lengths people go to watch the team, getting up first thing in the morning or travelling long distances. I try to get the fans involved through Twitter and Facebook, getting a good bit of banter going before kick-off and doing shout-outs throughout the show.

At Celtic, we are continually trying to speak to the fans and making it more informal. During the week, I will put tweets out on Twitter ranging from quiz questions to pictures I have taken around the stadium. People seem to really enjoy that, particularly fans who live abroad and haven't been here in quite a while.

We also film special features for the show. For example, in the lead-up to the Juventus game and the Scottish Cup final, we brought in some former players such as Dom Sullivan and Tommy Callaghan. I really enjoy hearing their perspective as you get an insight in to what it's like sitting in the dressing room before these big games. You have to pinch yourself sometimes, as these are the guys you saw as a fan or someone your Dad or uncle used to speak about. And the best part of it all is that they are just lovely people.

It was quite surreal when I started, particularly coming in halfway through the season. In my previous job, I had been filming fans in the fanzone before the Barcelona game, but I couldn't get a ticket for the game and ended up watching the game in a bar with my friend. And a few months later I was in the commentary booth working at the Juventus game. That was quite strange, but I managed to acclimatise.

The most enjoyable part of the job is the matches. You walk from the studio to the press box and after a couple of minutes you seem to switch off from your responsibilities as a presenter and just watch and talk about a game of football. It's also the funniest part of the job – maintaining that balance between being a fan and being professional! I will never forget the squeal I let out when Samaras scored that last-gasp winner against Aberdeen – the worst part was it won Goal of the Month so it was replayed constantly! A close second behind working at the games is speaking to the former players.

To see Kenny report all the latest news and action on *Celtic TV*, check out www.celticfc.tv

CELTIC TV

MATCHDAY MEMORIES...

WE thought we'd take a look at some Paradise programmes from down through the decades to see how the covers have changed through the seasons.

You may not recognise many of these, but they may bring back many memories for your parents – or even your grandparents.

These are only a few of the many Celtic matchday programme designs since the 1960s.

1977

SCOTTISH CUP

Sunday, 27th February, 1...

v Ayr United

KICK-OFF 3 p.m.

PROGRAMME 10p

1963

CELTIC
Official Programme

Bobby Murdoch

SCOTTISH LEAGUE – DIVISION 1
CELTIC v. ABERDEEN
Saturday, 12th October, 1963
Kick-off 3.00 p.m.

PRICE THREEPENCE

1970

OFFICIAL PROGRAMME
PRICE - SIXPENCE

CELTIC
v.
ST. MIRREN

LEAGUE CHAMPIONSHIP
Nov... 28, 1970

1973

Celtic Football & Athletic Co. Ltd.
FOUNDED 1888

DIRECTORS
Desmond White, C.A. (Chairman)
Thomas L. Devlin,
James M. Farrell, M.A., LL.B.
Kevin Kelly
MANAGER
John Stein, C.B.E.
OFFICIAL ADDRESS
Celtic Park, 95 Kerrydale Street,
Glasgow, S.E. Telephone: 041-554 2710

Celtic v. Rang...
CELTIC PARK

LEAGUE CUP
Saturday, 25th August 1973 Kick...

1982

CELTIC

PREMIER LEAGUE   CELTIC PARK   30p
DUNDEE
...OFF 1982 KICK-OFF 3.00 p.m.

1980

CELTIC
VERSUS
ABERDEEN

SCOTTISH PREMIER LEAGUE

CELTIC PARK

WED APRIL 23 1980

1980

Scottish Premier League

Celtic
versus MORTON

CELTIC PARK

Saturday ...th August 1980
...ick-off 3pm

...gramme
30p

1985

FINE FARE LEAGUE

Official Programme
Price 40p

CELTIC

versus
Rangers

1986

CELTIC
v Dumbarton
Skol Cup Third Round
Wednesday, August 27, 1986
Celtic Park, Glasgow
Kick-off 7.30 pm
Official programme 50p

COLOUR ME IN!

DEFENDER Emilio Izaguirre is about to tee up another scoring chance with a cross and we want you to get out your crayons, ink markers or paints and bring this image to full Celtic technicolour.

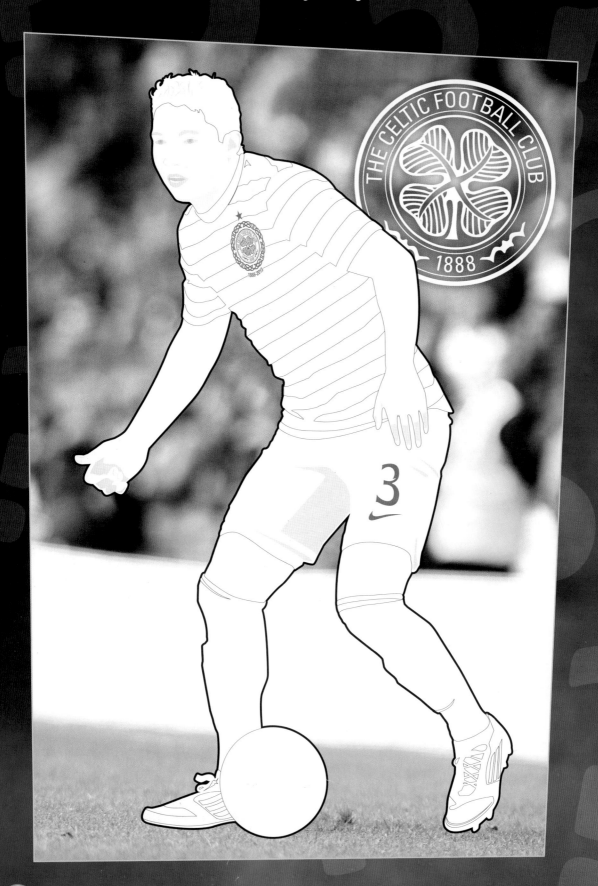

GUESS WHO?

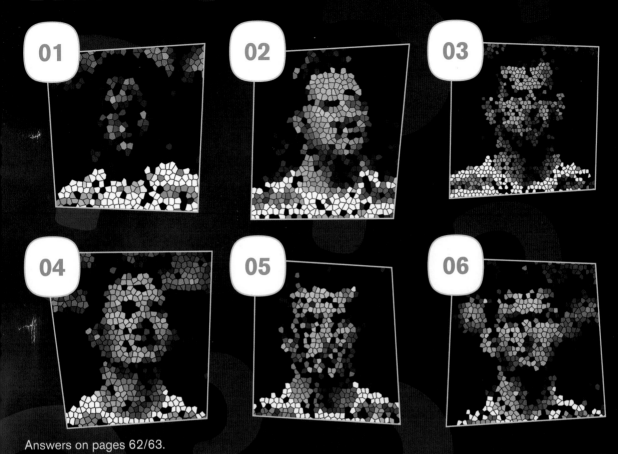

01 **02** **03**

04 **05** **06**

Answers on pages 62/63.

Manager's Office

Home Dressing Room

DOUBLE DEBUTS... AS PLAYER AND MANAGER

JIMMY McGRORY'S debut as a player was against Third Lanark away in a 1-0 league defeat on January 20, 1923. As manager, it was against Morton away in the wartime A Division in a 1-1 draw with 18,000 seeing Jackie Gallacher score Celtic's goal.

NEIL LENNON'S debut as a player was against Dundee away in the league in a 2-1 win, with goals by Stiliyan Petrov and Didier Agathe on December 10, 2000. As manager, it was against Kilmarnock in a 3-1 league win on March 27, 2010, with goals by Robbie Keane (2) and Scott Brown.

LOU MACARI'S debut as a player was against Ayr United away in the League Cup in a 2-0 win on September 27, 1967, with goals by Jim Brogan and Willie Wallace. As manager, it was against Rangers away in the league on October 30, 1993, in a 2-1 win, with goals by John Collins and Brian O'Neil watched by 47,522.

JIMMY McSTAY'S debut as a player was against Clyde away in a 1-0 league win on November 4, 1922, with Jean McFarlane scoring in front of 13,000. As manager, it was against Kilmarnock away in the wartime Western Division in a 3-2 defeat, with goals by John Gould and John Divers on February 17, 1940.

EUROVISION

THE second part of our continental Q&A with two more Bhoys on the hot seat giving their answers.

Joe Ledley

First European match?

It was Braga away from home in the Champions League qualifier a few years ago. We lost 3-0 on the night so it wasn't the greatest of starts!

Favourite European ground?

Barcelona, the atmosphere wasn't the best actually, but I had always wanted to play there ever since I was young.

A Champions League final you enjoyed watching?

I would have to say Liverpool against AC Milan in Istanbul, that's been the best final of recent years.

A European city you have played in with Celtic and would like to return to?

When we played against Ajax in pre-season, I thought Amsterdam was a really nice city.

A European team you have not faced but would like to play against?

Borussia Dortmund, as I would like to play at their ground. The atmosphere looks brilliant any time I have watched their games.

Hardest opponent you have come up against in Europe?

I am going to go for Andres Iniesta. I think he's just a brilliant player. He is two-footed, technically good, can go either side and can see a pass. I felt he was even better in real life than what you see on TV, and I don't feel he gets the credit he deserves. He's a really gifted player.

Greatest European game you have been involved in?

Barcelona at Celtic Park – we beat the best team in the world.

Adam Matthews

First European match?

I didn't play in any of the Sion games, so it was against Atletico Madrid away in the Europa League when I came on as a substitute.

Favourite European ground?

Juventus' ground. It felt like the stadium was on top of you and the atmosphere was brilliant.

A Champions League final you enjoyed watching?

Liverpool v AC Milan - to come back to win from being 3-0 down was amazing.

A European city you have played in with Celtic and would like to return to?

I thought Munich was decent when we were in Germany for pre-season. We had a chance to look around it and it had great scenery.

A European team you have not faced but would like to play against?

Bayern Munich – they are the best team in Europe at the minute and you always want to test yourself against the best players and teams.

Hardest opponent you have come up against in Europe?

Ronaldo. We played against Real Madrid in a friendly last year and you just never knew what he was going to do – left-foot, right-foot. He was just fantastic.

Greatest European game you have been involved in?

Winning against Barcelona was brilliant, and the atmosphere was incredible.

Celtic Soccer Skills School

Learn the tricks of the trade from the best in the business.

GOALKEEPING – FRASER FORSTER

A GOOD goalkeeper is fundamental for successful sides. It's the most specialised position in the team and it takes special skill and dedication to play at the highest level.

Having a safe pair of hands in the last line of defence instils confidence throughout the rest of the team. In Fraser Forster, Celtic have one of the best in the business.

The Englishman had an outstanding season between the sticks for the Bhoys. His most memorable moment came in the 2-1 victory over Barcelona when a heroic performance saw him described as 'La Grand Muralla' (The Great Wall) in the Spanish press.

Displays like that saw him earn a call-up to the full England squad, underlining his status as one of the finest shot-stoppers in the UK. Want to follow in his foot-steps? Then follow his guidance for budding goalies.

Shot-stopping

The key one is to be set when people are shooting. Make sure you are not moving as if you are it's very hard to make a save. By remaining still and keeping your head still when someone shoots, it makes it a lot easier. It's important you get a good push off into your dive. If you do decide to parry the shot, it's vital you direct the ball wide and away from the goal.

One-on-ones

It depends on where the player is. If he is through one-on-one, you have to stay away from the ball until he has reached a reasonable point. Then you obviously spread yourself as big as you can and get as close as you can to the striker as this narrows the angle and the amount of goal he is able to see. It also helps to stay on your feet as well as it makes it harder for him to go round you and you might force him into making a mistake or get a chance to get a touch on the ball

Dealing with crosses

Just to stay in position until you have made your decision. Don't pre-guess where the ball is going and stay until you know the flight of the ball. The important thing is not to move until you know this and then you make your decision – you either stay or you go as fast as you can and try and collect the ball at its highest point. If you go for it, you have to get a touch on the ball.

Distribution

It's probably the biggest thing for the modern goalkeeper now. If you are dealing with a back-pass, you need to know what you are doing with the ball before you get it. That means knowing who you are going to pass it to, and if you are under pressure, preparing to kick it long – you can't take any chances either. You have to be positive in your decision-making and then execute the pass.

Communication

Obviously a goalkeeper can see a full pitch so it's important that you talk to your back four as much as you can as the game is going on, just giving out simple information and helping them out as best you can. You should also let them know that you are ready for the ball or coming to collect it so they will leave it for you.

Saving a penalty

It's just instinct really. You don't dive too early so the penalty taker can't see where you are going. It's also important to make yourself as big as you can as psychologically it might help. If you slow down the taking of the penalty it might give the striker more time to think about it and it puts them under a bit more pressure.

General advice

Just to work as hard as you can at everything you do in training as you will improve rapidly. There is always extra stuff you can do. You can always get better no matter the level you are playing at, so keep giving it absolutely everything and if it doesn't work out for some reason, you can at least look back and think that you gave it your all.

DOUBLE DELIGHT:
TOP TEAM'S TWIN TROPHY TIME

DOUBLE DELIGHT:
TOP TEAM'S TWIN TROPHY TIME

Celtic mark their 125th Anniversary in silverware style

SEASON 2012/13 was a roaring success on many fronts for Neil Lennon and his young team as they drove themselves on to the championship and the Scottish Cup for a memorable and historic double.

...marking that achievement, the Irishman became the third Celtic ...end to lift the double both as player and manager when he ...ulated the feats of Hoops giants Jock Stein and Billy McNeill.

...ed, Caesar lifted the double as manager in the club's ...enary year and Neil Lennon did likewise as the club ...orated it's 125th Anniversary and the marking of that ...stone in the club's history delivered another memorable night ...veryone with Celtic at heart.

...ecial event was held at St Mary's Church in the Calton, the ...lace of Celtic Football Club, and among the dignitaries ...on the night were the directors of Barcelona – the Hoops' ...g partners 24 hours later in the UEFA Champions League.

And, as you may know, Celtic marked their birthday in the best possible way by beating the best team in the world 2-1 at Paradise thanks to goals from Victor Wanyama and Tony Watt.

The Hoops, of course, went on to qualify for the last 16 of the tournament before losing out to Juventus, but, as memorable as that run was, the season was all about silverware on the domestic front and the Hoops delivered their 15th League and Scottish Cup double.

The championship was clinched with five games left to play as Celtic racked up a 4-1 win over the visiting Inverness Caledonian Thistle and three weeks later in the Hoops' next home game, a 4-0 win over St Johnstone preceded the presentation of the trophy.

All eyes were then on the final game of the season as Celtic lined up against Hibernian at Hampden in the Scottish Cup final where a 3-0 win rounded off the club's 125th Anniversary season in the best possible way.

See if you can match up the Celtic player with the club from which he signed:

01	Henrik Larsson	01	Derby County
02	Neil Lennon	02	Rosenborg
03	Kris Commons	03	Ashdod
04	John Hartson	04	Aberdeen
05	Mikael Lustig	05	Nottingham Forest
06	Fraser Forster	06	Leicester City
07	Efe Ambrose	07	Chelsea
08	Charlie Mulgrew	08	Feyenoord
09	Kelvin Wilson	09	Newcastle United
10	Chris Sutton	10	Coventry City

Answers on pages 62/63.

Manager's Office

Home Dressing Room

DOUBLE DEBUTS...
AS PLAYER AND MANAGER

WILLIE MALEY played in Celtic's first ever game when they beat Rangers 5-2 at home on May 28, 1888, but his competitive debut was against Cowlairs in an 8-0 Scottish Cup win on September 22, 1888, watched by 6,500. His first game as Secretary/Manager was a 4-1 home league win against Hibernian, watched by 17,000 on September 4, 1897. His first game solely as manager was on August 17, 1918, in a 3-0 away league win against Hibernian, watched by 15,000.

TONY MOWBRAY'S debut as a player was against Aberdeen in the league on November 9, 1991, at home in a 2-1 win with goals by Charlie Nicholas and Gerry Creaney watched by a crowd of 36,387. As manager, it was against Moscow Dynamo in the Champions League on July 29, 2009, in a 1-0 home defeat.

DOUBLE DELIGHT: MAY THE FOURTH BE WITH YOU

Celtic's Youth Academy wrap up an amazing quadruple double

CELTIC Under-20s had another season to savour as they won the league and cup double for the fourth successive year.

Achieving the 'quadruple double' was a fantastic feat for the entire Celtic Youth Academy, highlighting the abundance of talent that is continuing to progress through the system.

The ultimate aim of the club's youth set-up is bringing players through to the top-team and four more made their debut for Neil Lennon's side during the 2012/13 season – Joe Chalmers, Jackson Irvine, Bahrudin Atajic and John Herron.

But an important part of their development as a Celtic player is becoming adept at winning silverware and they deserve huge credit for this latest round of success.

Despite a change in the structure of the Pro-Youth system in Scotland, which saw the Under-19 league reverting to an Under-20 competition, the young Bhoys showed they were still the team to beat as they made a storming start to the season, winning five games on the spin.

By the halfway point in the campaign, Stevie Frail and John Kennedy's side were well-positioned to take charge in the title race, and a long

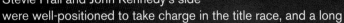

unbeaten run left their rivals trailing in their wake. The finishing line was soon in sight.

Just three days after the first-team sealed the SPL championship, the youths travelled to Inverness on April 24, knowing a victory in the Highlands would seal the crown.

It looked as though the champagne would need to be put on ice as the game remained goal-less entering its 90th minute. However, James Keatings stepped up and scored a spectacular free-kick with practically the last kick of the ball to start the celebrations.

That allowed the young Hoops to turn their attentions to the SFA Youth Cup final the following week, with Dunfermline standing between them and a historic double.

Both sides failed to find the net in a hard-fought first half at Hampden but the Bhoys stepped up the pace to take charge after the interval. Jamie Lindsay opened the scoring and a fine header from top scorer Atajic doubled their advantage.

Although the Fifers quickly reduced the deficit, Denny Johnstone's late finish ensured the cup would be joining the league trophy in Paradise for the fourth year running.

Celtic Soccer Skills School

Learn the tricks of the trade from the best in the business.

STRIKING TIPS – ANTHONY STOKES

GOALS win football matches and ultimately silverware. This makes prolific strikers the most prized possessions in football and iconic figures among supporters.

An array of fantastic forwards have lined up for Celtic throughout their history including Jimmy McGrory, Kenny Dalglish and Henrik Larsson.

One of the latest to achieve success is Anthony Stokes, who has averaged around a goal every two games since joining the Hoops in 2011. In that time, Celtic have won successive league championships and two Scottish Cups.

Many elements are involved in the art of goalscoring and here the Irishman passes on some pointers in becoming a successful striker.

Shooting

My touch dictates where I put the ball. If it's underneath my feet there is not a lot I can do. Nine time out of 10, your touch sets you up for a shot, especially if you are in a tight position. Get it right and you can get the ball in front of you and a clean strike at goal. It's important to try and put it in the corner with power. A lot of times, though, it's a split second decision. Sometimes you look at the keeper to see what position he is in. The main thing is to always strike it across the keeper. Even if he manages to save it, you are expecting someone being there to tap it in.

Through on goal

Composure is important. Don't rush it. Figure it out in your mind, before picking your spot and then go for it – don't change your mind as you tend to scuff or drag your shot. A lot of times, the keeper will show you one side of the goal and will almost gamble. You also have the option of going round the keeper. He will always come out to try and narrow his angles. If you have enough time and are clear

one-on-one, it can be easier to take a touch around him and then it can be quite simple.

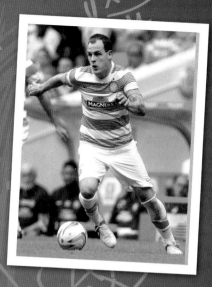

Movement

If I want the ball short, I will move as if am going to run in behind the defender and then come off and show to feet. This normally gives me a yard or two. If you want to run in behind the defence, you do the opposite – look like you are coming to get the ball to feet, spin and then go. It's something I do quite a bit. I'm not lightning fast, but that movement can give you the split second you need. Always try and drag the defender in the opposite direction to where you want the ball.

Positioning

It's a partnership when you play up front. You have to try and have a good understanding with your strike partner. When I played alongside Gary Hooper, I tended to be the one that played up highest while he sat in the hole. My job was to try and keep the two centre halves occupied up the pitch to give him space. On the other hand, if a defender tried to close him down, it gave me a chance to spin off and get in behind. It worked well naturally, as he liked to sit deeper while I preferred to stretch the defence.

Defending from the front

Probably something that has only really come into my game since I arrived here. I wasn't the best at it until I was 19 or 20, but then I realised if you want to play at the top level that everyone in the team needs to work – and that starts with the strikers. You can't go off like a loose cannon, chasing the ball on your own. People need to dictate from behind you, where to press and where they want the ball to go. Sometimes I will hear the midfield behind me asking to let them come inside as they are close enough to put pressure on the ball there and other times they will ask me to show a player down the line. It's one of those things where everyone needs to communicate.

Heading the ball

I don't score many headers, maybe one or two a season. It's something I need to work on. After coming back from my injury, I was physically stronger and that's helped my game in the air as you need to have strength when challenging big defenders. You need to compete and try and win headers so the ball isn't constantly coming back.

An important tip improve your game

As a kid, I couldn't use my left foot but now I would never shy away from taking something on my left foot and having a crack. That was down to all my hard work I put in when I was only eight or nine and starting out in football. My dad probably had a big part to play in that. He used to tell me to only use my left foot in training sessions so for a few hours that is all I would do. I practiced relentlessly on it and now I might score five or six goals a season on my left foot.

SCOTTISH CUP FINAL MEDIA DAY

In the days leading up to the Scottish Cup final victory over Hibernian, Celtic held a media day at the club's Lennoxtown training base, and we went behind the scenes to reveal what happens when the cameras start rolling and the microphones are switched on.

DOUBLE VISION

Cameras from the nation's major TV stations film shots of Mikael Lustig with the cup which will be shown on the day's sports bulletins.

PICTURE PERFECT

Then it's time for the press photographers to catch the Swede in their lens for the snap that will make the next day's back pages.

QUESTION TIME

The Swedish defender answers a range of questions from broadcast journalists on the cup final.

FORREST IN FOCUS

The Celtic wing-wizard is next to step into the hot seat and give his thoughts to the assembled media on the Hampden showpiece.

COMMONS TOUCH

It's Kris Commons' turn to be snapped with the trophy at Celtic's training base against the backdrop of Lennox Castle.

GREEN DAY

Anthony Stokes speaks in front of the cameras at the prospect of facing his former employers in the Scottish Cup final.

STOP PRESS

The Irishman moves to a different room where he's quizzed by reporters from the daily newspapers on the big game.

CLUB CALL

Away from all the hullaballoo, Celtic TV's Gerry McDade sits down with Kris Commons in one of the dressing rooms to chat about the prospect of a domestic double.

THE FINAL OUTCOME

The Scottish Cup is on its way back to Paradise for the 36th time.

MAZE (Page 26)